Cuent@

poems by

Pablo Miguel Martínez

Finishing Line Press
Georgetown, Kentucky

Cuent@

Copyright © 2016 by Pablo Miguel Martínez
ISBN 978-1-944899-03-5 First Edition
All rights reserved under International and Pan-American Copyright Conventions. No part of this book may be reproduced in any manner whatsoever without written permission from the publisher, except in the case of brief quotations embodied in critical articles and reviews.

ACKNOWLEDGMENTS

"Deed" was originally published as a limited-edition letterpress-printed broadside at the Center for Book Arts in New York.

Editor: Christen Kincaid

Cover Art: Nido de las águilas, Tijuana, Baja California, México, 1996; ©Elsa Medina

Author Photo: ©Henry M. Cantú

Cover Design: Elizabeth Maines

Printed in the USA on acid-free paper.
Order online: www.finishinglinepress.com
   also available on amazon.com

Author inquiries and mail orders:
Finishing Line Press
P. O. Box 1626
Georgetown, Kentucky 40324
U. S. A.

Table of Contents

Preludio 1

Article X 2

Xing 3

Tempo: Rubato 4

Debt 5

Gloria 6

A/cento: Un sueño 7

Un documento 8

The *I* in Dos 9

Script 10

Deed 11

& tortillas dreaming 12

Traje de tierra 13

Cuento 15

Cuenta 19

Unearthed 21

For my father, Pablo Martínez, whose work shapes all my cuentos.
And for all the unknown—may their dignity be restored.

Who made them serfs of the soil?
—*Henry David Thoreau*

Preludio

Empieza por ti, she says.
So I start with tierra—
Dirt. Earth. Dust. Land.
And since I have started
With dirt, I am dirty,
As in "dirty Mexican,"
As in "filthy Mexican."
In Mexican, they say,
Diaspora means you die
As poor as you started.
[Rim shot] Gun shot.
Dirt poor we are—bereft
Of land, dispossessed.
This is my inheritance:
To labor in fields
Where rivulets of sweat
Are the headwaters
Of our fate.

Article X [stricken out]

When the U.S. Senate reluctantly ratified the Treaty of Guadalupe Hidalgo on March 10, 1848, it deleted Article X, which guaranteed the protection of Mexican land grants.

Xing

I wait to make the sign
Of the tilted cross—
Under the fan's tireless
Blading I wait to make
My mark. I will be paid
Fairly, they say. Well tamed
Rows of silent brown men,
Sweaty, dirty from labors
Ripened by seasons of betrayal.
Our X's, leaning crosses,
Are not the eyes of the besotted.
Crosses [double beams], brought
Down to rest on parcels
Of untilled wisdom, left to rot
By the beaming patrón
Who unfolds the document
Waiting for my *X*.

Tempo: Rubato

Here we are unprotected,
We are ever vulnerable, running
All ways for cover, for wages,
For that thing they call dignity.
God's ancient eyelids, thin
As the tomatillo's husk,
Are shut. He doesn't see.
Don't tell me about miracles.
Don't tell me about the indio's
Tilma. To be left alone,
Undetected, undisturbed—
That would be a florid blessing,
Señor. It would be enough.
But that will come only
When I am laid in earth.

When I am laid in earth,
May my wrongs create
No trouble, no trouble
In thy breast.

["When I am laid in Earth" is an aria from Henry Purcell's opera "Dido and Aeneas" (1689). *Rubato* denotes a free-flowing tempo, literally, "robbed."]

Debt

Hijo, I did not speak—
but it wasn't weakness, ¿entiendes?

So much had been broken.
And when la gente was rent—

shattered like so many bones—
they set us one against the other,

¿entiendes? The papers, the promises,
all meaningless, ¿entiendes? Our past

meant nothing. Only our bodies for labor,
for lust. *Padre nuestro*, I prayed.

You must learn these words, they said.
But what good are words when they say

equal and leave us to burn? It doesn't
dampen el hambre. My heart says we are

equal, yes. *Forgive us our debts, as we forgive
our debtors.* Is the word's true meaning

in the patrón's not paying us
what we are due? Is it his denying us

a warm bed when the earth sleeps,
and cool water when it blooms?

This word, *debt*, sounds too much
like that other one, ¿entiendes? ¿Entiendes?

Gloria

Nuestros labores—works, opera.
Domingo Arias' lettuce, ruffled—not
Closed tight, like the patrón's heart.
The heads flare and flounce,
Faldas on a Saturday night
Back in Jalapa, where Domingo
Met Gloria, where his head
Filled with thoughts of *nuestro,*
Nosotros—us! How the words
Played in the crisp night breeze,
A sympathetic vibrating—chords
Echoing in these well-scored
surcos del corazón.

[The Italian word *opera* means "works."]

A/cento: Un sueño

I see myself, but from the outside
Beneath veneers of sweat and soot, clothes reeking
I wait for you by the burning road
At first, the friendly timbre of the voices
There's a train whistle too. In and out like this.
And each singer cried more than sang
Me sacaron de los montes donde desnudé la tierra.
Where the light is, and each thing clear,
With an eye we lift up the peach tree.
What drives us out *into the four corners of the known world?*
Looking back, we cannot see,
Aquí venimos a colgar nuestras caras.
The wind stirred faintly, there was nothing more.

Un documento

Mexicans! Many of you have been robbed
of your property, incarcerated, chased,
murdered, and hunted like wild beasts,
because your labor was fruitful, and because
your industry excited the vile avarice
which led them.

—Juan N. Cortina
Cameron County, Texas
November 23, 1859

The *I* in Dos

At my birth there was a great gushing,
A brown river swollen by the riving,

A scream that split Before from
After—Them from Us.

Empieza por ti, she says. Empieza.
So I start.

I am the shame and the need
Of imported arms, bracero.

I am the dry well and the spume
Of their lasciviousness, mujer.

I am the meager meal
And the fattened pride, niño.

I am the supporting beam
And the angry graffito

Of liberty's flat façade,
The silt and the pearl

In history's unruly sea.
Empieza por ti, she said.

Script

We really stole Texas, didn't we, Mr. Benedict?
I mean, away from Mexico.

[…]

They took it off a bunch of ignorant Mexicans.

—Dialogue from the movie "Giant"

Deed

This land
        Say *rez*
This land
        Say *barrio*
This land
        Say *township*
This land
        Say *favela*
This land
        Say *camp*
This land
        Say *underpass*
This land
        Say *colony*
This land
        Say *ghetto*
This land
        Was made
For you—
        Para ti, hijo

& tortillas dreaming

My mind cannot be prisoned
on their peñasco. It will leap, ¿ves?
My thoughts will never be
perimetered by soulless charting, ¿entiendes?
My thoughts rage and roam like Apache
ponies, unbridled; like wild
plants, they thrive, the poisonous
and the healing ones. Autochthonous,
the scholars call us—aboriginal.
Here, on this land, long before their
letters and their thieving, mi razón
rooted, flowered, seeded, spread far—
yes, farther—than their light
eyes could ever hope to see.

[The title is taken from "Howl" by Allen Ginsberg.]

Traje de tierra

My suit of dust, folded
In my lungs, bolsas llenas
De sufrimiento. Filled
With brown penny songs.
So much pentimento,
Mi'jo. Esta es mi tierra.
Mi gloria. Here, for you—
This land.

*come celebrate / with me that everyday /
something has tried to kill me / and has failed.*
    —*Lucille Clifton*

Cuento

> *En Tres Ríos sucedió,*
> *en los tiempos de la guerra,*
> *Félix Longoria murió*
> *peleando por esta tierra.*
> —South Texas corrido

In 1945, Pvt. Felix Longoria, a native of Three Rivers, Texas, was killed in action by a sniper's bullet on the island of Luzon.

■

Four years he lay in obsidian-flecked archipelago clay, alejado de la tierra madre. No mourning there, only cooing of fruit doves on that island, faraway. Each night his young wife lay in their Three Rivers bed, a strange braid of dread, pain, and memory on her pillow. *Come home, corazón*, she'd plead, his absence a phantom limb that worried her sleep. But what remains is never easy—the known and the unknown, the truth shining slant, like dim winter light.

■

According to several sources, the only funeral home in Three Rivers refused Pvt. Longoria's remains. "I can't let his body rest at this chapel because the whites won't like it," the owner said. "You know how the Latin people get drunk and lay around all the time," he said. "We never let Latins use the chapel and we don't intend to start now."

■

The state of Texas, which looms so large on the map,
certainly looks small tonight.
    —Walter Winchell

■

They predict a long battle, Felix.
So many wrongs, mi amor. I fear

we'll never find peace, you and me.
But for you I'm strong. It's funny:

we fight to stop the fighting. Más
pleito, hermana says. From dust

you came, and to dust you'll return,
the priest said. But this dust—esta tierra

tejana—doesn't want you. I am denied
a few hours of undammed wailing—my

Mexicanness on display—the whites
wouldn't like that. So loud and hard,

all our wars, ¿no? The last sound
you heard—a shot on that volcano island.

Ay, I pray you weren't alone. Aquí en Tejas
I am learning to speak—each plea

a bright eruption. Mi coraje—
courage and rage, corazón. You

would be proud, Felix. Tonight
there is no trouble in my breast,

only the wide, wild hueco that is me
without you.

■

A then-young U.S. Senator from Texas, Lyndon B. Johnson, intervened, and Pvt. Felix Longoria was buried in Arlington National Cemetery. The funeral took place on February 16, 1949.

■

Later that year, the Texas House of Representatives formed a Special Committee on the Reburial of Felix Longoria. The Committee concluded that no racial discrimination had taken place. This was never incorporated into the legislative record. The records of the Committee, cited in a majority report, "are not held at the State Archives, and their whereabouts are unknown," according to the Texas State Historical Assn.

■

Arlington National Cemetery is 1,600 miles from Three Rivers.

■

Forever you'll be so far
from me, Felix—alejado
de tu tierra. Who will
watch over you, querido?

Cuenta

> "A mass grave of unidentified migrants was uncovered in Brooks County, Texas. Anthropologists working at the site found many instances of multiple bodies in trash bags, bones in shopping bags or simply buried in the dirt. The anthropologists were working at Sacred Heart Burial Park in Falfurrias, Texas. [...] According to county officials, a local funeral home, Funeraria del Angel, was paid $450 per body to handle the migrants found by local law-enforcement officials."
> —article in the *International Business Times*, June 21, 2014

Who are these scabbed seraphs
That watch over the atrocity—
Who, dry-eyed and eager,
Build another city of pain,
Grouted with their mix of
Ash and tears? Stripped
Of gilt harps, they pluck
The souls of campesinos
To the unforgiving beat
Of death-rattles—dried,
Hollow gourds. Their
Diaphanous garb charred
By hellish flame, they wear
Robes sewn in rancid rooms.

In God we trust, they say.
But his messengers arrived
With trash bags, shopping bags—
No dignity in this. [*Dignity*,
from the Latin for "worth"]
So they sang their glad tidings
in these forsaken scapes. So we

Were returned to dust, dressed
In the attire of refuse, of dirt.
So we were laid in earth. His sacred
Heart didn't bleed. It throbbed wantonly,
A crossing signal for their crowded
Wagons, chuffing their way to eternity.
The fare: a filthy four-hundred fifty.

Unearthed

> *Colorín colorado, este cuento se ha acabado.*
> —*popular Spanish phrase at the end of stories*

What to call a story that's never done?
Cuento sin fin, engraved, unremitting rhyme.
Dust-to-dust toil, never finished, just begun.

In unceasing cycles of season and sun,
Thick debts batter too-thin dimes.
What to call a story that's never done?

A fable with no moral, authored by no one,
Migration in dust-jacketed dreamtime,
Dust-to-dust toil, never finished, just begun.

Cuenta el cuento, hijo—tell it with conviction,
Rip cheap fictions. Erase hate-hatched signs.
What shall we call this story that's never done?

Go home, they'll tell you, thinking you'll run.
Empieza por ti: rewrite the plotless storyline.
Dust-to-dust toil, never finished, just begun.

I wish you a life of unsoiled work, my son,
Far from clipped angels and their earthly crime.
What should we call this story that's never done?
Dust-to-dust toil, never finished, just begun.

Pablo Miguel Martínez is the author of the collection *Brazos, Carry Me* (Kórima Press), which received the 2013 PEN Southwest Book Award for Poetry. His work has appeared in numerous literary journals, newspapers, and anthologies, including *Best Gay Poetry 2008, Borderlands: Texas Poetry Review, El Paso Times, Gay and Lesbian Review, North American Review, Pilgrimage, San Antonio Express-News* and *This Assignment Is So Gay*. Martínez has been a recipient of the Robert L.B. Tobin Award for Artistic Excellence, the Oscar Wilde Award, and the Chicano/Latino Literary Prize. His literary work has received support from the Alfredo Cisneros Del Moral Foundation and the Artist Foundation of San Antonio.

Martínez is a Co-Founder of CantoMundo, a national retreat-workshop for Latina/o poets. He lives in San Antonio, Texas.

www.ingramcontent.com/pod-product-compliance
Lightning Source LLC
Chambersburg PA
CBHW060226050426
42446CB00013B/3197